Old Indian Days
Part Two
The Woman

by

Charles A. Eastman

Double9 BOOKS

Old Indian Days
Part Two
The Woman
by Charles A. Eastman

ISBN: 978-93-64289-10-8

Published by

DOUBLE 9 BOOKS
2/13-B, Ansari Road
Daryaganj, New Delhi – 110002
info@double9books.com
www.double9books.com
Tel. 011-40042856

ABOUT THE AUTHOR

Charles Alexander Eastman (1858-1939), also known as Hakadah and later as Ohiyesa, was a prominent Native American author, physician, and activist. He was born in a Dakota Sioux community near Redwood Falls, Minnesota, to a mixed-race family of Dakota and European descent. Orphaned at an early age during the Dakota War of 1862, Eastman was raised in the traditional Dakota Sioux manner until the age of 15, when he attended formal schooling in the East. Eastman went on to become one of the first Native Americans to graduate from medical school, earning his medical degree from Boston University in 1889. He dedicated much of his life to advocating for Native American rights and education, working as a physician on reservations and serving as a government Indian inspector. Eastman is best known for his writings that aimed to preserve and promote understanding of Native American culture and history. His works include several books such as "Indian Boyhood" (1902), "Old Indian Days" (1907), and "The Soul of the Indian" (1911), which were instrumental in shaping non-Native perceptions of Native American life and spirituality. These books often drew from his personal experiences and upbringing, offering insights into traditional Dakota Sioux customs, spirituality, and values.

Charles A. Eastman's legacy extends beyond his literary contributions; he played a significant role in bridging cultural divides and promoting dialogue between Native and non-Native communities. His writings continue to be studied for their historical significance and their role in preserving Native American heritage.

CONTENTS

I
WINONA, THE WOMAN-CHILD

Hush, hushaby, little woman!
Be brave and weep not!
The spirits sleep not;
'Tis they who ordain
To woman, pain.

Hush, hushaby, little woman!
Now, all things bearing,
A new gift sharing
From those above—

To woman, love.
—Sioux Lullaby.

"Chinto, weyanna! Yes, indeed; she is a real little woman," declares the old grandmother, as she receives and critically examines the tiny bit of humanity.

There is no remark as to the color of its hair or eyes, both so black as almost to be blue, but the old woman scans sharply the delicate profile of the baby face.

"Ah, she has the nose of her ancestors! Lips thin as a leaf, and eyes bright as stars in midwinter!" she exclaims, as she passes on the furry bundle to the other grandmother for her inspection.

"Tokee! she is pretty enough to win a twinkle rom the evening star," remarks that smiling personage.

"And what shall her name be?

"Winona, the First-born, of course. That is hers by right of birth."

"Still, it may not fit her. One must prove herself worthy in order to retain that honorable name."

"Ugh," retorts the first grandmother, "she can at least bear it on probation!"

"Tosh, tosh," the other assents.

Thus the unconscious little Winona has passed the first stage of the Indian's christening.

Presently she is folded into a soft white doeskin, well lined with the loose down of cattails, and snugly laced into an upright oaken cradle, the front of which is a richly embroidered buckskin bag, with porcupine quills and deers' hoofs suspended from its profuse fringes. This gay cradle is strapped upon the second grandmother's back, and that dignitary walks off with the newcomer.

"You must come with me," she says. "We shall go among the father and mother trees, and hear them speak with their thousand tongues, that you may know their language forever. I will hang the cradle of the woman-child upon Utuhu, the oak; and she shall hear the love-sighs of the pine maiden!"

In this fashion Winona is introduced to nature and becomes at once "nature-born," in accord with the beliefs and practices of the wild red man.

"Here she is! Take her," says the old woman on her return from the woods. She presents the child to its mother, who is sitting in the shade of an elm-tree as quietly as if she had not just passed through woman's severest ordeal in giving a daughter to the brave Chetonska!

"She has a winsome face, as meek and innocent as the face of an ermine," graciously adds the grandmother.

The mother does not speak. Silently and almost reverently she takes her new and first-born daughter into her arms. She gazes into its velvety little face of a dusky red tint, and unconsciously presses the closely swaddled form to her breast. She feels the mother-instinct seize upon her strongly for the first time. Here is a new life, a new hope, a possible link between herself and a new race!

Ah, a smile plays upon her lips, as she realizes that she has kissed her child! In its eyes and mouth she discerns clearly the features she has loved in the strong countenance of another, though in the little woman's face they are softened and retouched by the hand of the "Great Mystery."

The baby girl is called Winona for some months, when the medicine-man is summoned and requested to name publicly the first-born daughter of Chetonska, the White Hawk; but not until he has received a present of a good pony with a finely painted buffalo-robe. It is usual to confer another name besides that of the "First-born," which may be resumed later if the maiden proves worthy. The name Winona implies much of honor. It means charitable, kind, helpful; all that an eldest sister should be!

The herald goes around the ring of lodges announcing in singsong fashion the christening, and inviting everybody to a feast in honor of the event. A real American christening is always a gala occasion, when much savage wealth is distributed among the poor and old people. Winona has only just walked, and this fact is also announced with additional gifts. A wellborn child is ever before the tribal eye and in the tribal ear, as every little step in its progress toward manhood or womanhood—the first time of walking or swimming, first shot with bow and arrow (if a boy), first pair of moccasins made (if a girl)—is announced publicly with feasting and the giving of presents.

So Winona receives her individual name of Tatiyopa, or Her Door. It is symbolic, like most Indian names, and implies that the door of the bearer is hospitable and her home attractive.

The two grandmothers, who have carried the little maiden upon their backs, now tell and sing to her by turns all the legends of their most noted female ancestors, from the twin sisters of the old story, the maidens who married among the star people of the sky, down to their own mothers. All her lullabies are feminine, and designed to impress upon her tender mind the life and duties of her sex.

As soon as she is old enough to play with dolls she plays mother in all seriousness and gravity. She is dressed like a miniature woman (and her dolls are clad likewise), in garments of doeskin to her ankles, adorned with long fringes, embroidered with porcupine quills, and dyed with root dyes in various colors. Her little blanket or robe, with which she shyly drapes or screens her head and shoulders, is the skin of a buffalo calf or a deer, soft, white, embroidered on the smooth side, and often with the head and hoofs left on.

"You must never forget, my little daughter, that you are a woman like myself. Do always those things that you see me do," her mother often admonishes her.

Even the language of the Sioux has its feminine dialect, and the tiny girl would be greatly abashed were it ever needful to correct her for using a masculine termination.

This mother makes for her little daughter a miniature copy of every rude tool that she uses in her daily tasks. There is a little scraper of elk-horn to scrape rawhides preparatory to tanning them, another scraper of a different shape for tanning, bone knives, and stone mallets for pounding choke-cherries and jerked meat.

While her mother is bending over a large buffalo-hide stretched and pinned upon the ground, standing upon it and scraping off the fleshy portion as nimbly as a carpenter shaves a board with his plane, Winona, at five years of age, stands upon a corner of the great hide and industriously scrapes away with her tiny instrument! When the mother stops to sharpen her tool, the little woman always sharpens hers also. Perhaps there is water to be fetched in bags made from the dried pericardium of an animal; the girl brings some in a smaller water-bag. When her mother goes for wood she carries one or two sticks on her back. She pitches her play teepee to form an exact copy of her mother's. Her little belongings are nearly all practical, and her very play is real!

Thus, before she is ten years old, Winona begins to see life honestly and in earnest; to consider herself a factor in the life of her people—a link in the genealogy of her race. Yet her effort is not forced, her work not done from necessity; it is normal and a development of the play-instinct of the young creature. This sort of training leads very early to a genuine desire to serve and to do for others. The little Winona loves to give and to please; to be generous and gracious. There is no thought of trafficking or economizing in labor and in love.

"Mother, I want to be like the beavers, the ants, and the spiders, because my grandmother says those are the people most worthy of imitation for their industry. She also tells me that I should watch the bee, the one that has so many daughters, and allows no young men to come around her daughters while they are at work making sweets," exclaims the little maiden.

"Truly their industry helps us much, for we often take from their hoard," remarks the mother.

"That is not right, is it mother, if they do not wish to share with us?" asks Winona. "But I think the bee is stingy if she has so much and will not share with any one else! When I grow up, I shall help the poor! I shall have a big teepee and invite old people often, for when people get old they seem to be always hungry, and I think we ought to feed them."

"My little daughter will please me and her father if she proves to be industrious and skillful with her needle and in all woman's work. Then she can have a fine teepee and make it all cheerful within. The indolent woman has a small teepee, and it is very smoky. All her children will have sore eyes, and her husband will soon become ill-tempered," declares the mother, in all seriousness.

"And, daughter, there is something more than this needed to make a cheerful home. You must have a good heart, be patient, and speak but little. Every creature that talks too much is sure to make trouble," she concludes, wisely.

One day this careful mother has completed a beautiful little teepee of the skin of a buffalo calf, worked with red porcupine quills in a row of rings just below the smoke-flaps and on each side of the front opening. In the center of each ring is a tassel of red and white horse-hair. The tip of each smoke-flap is decorated with the same material, and the doorflap also.

Within there are neatly arranged raw-hide boxes for housekeeping, and square bags of soft buckskin adorned with blue and white beads. On either side of the fireplace are spread the tanned skins of a buffalo calf and a deer; but there is no bear, wolf, or wildcat skin, for on these the foot of a woman must never tread! They are for men, and symbolical of manly virtues. There are dolls of all sizes, and a play travois leans against the white wall of the miniature lodge. Even the pet pup is called in to complete the fanciful home of the little woman.

"Now, my daughter," says the mother, "you must keep your lodge in order!"

Here the little woman is allowed to invite other little women, her playmates. This is where the grandmothers hold sway, chaperoning their young charges, who must never be long out of their sight. The little visitors bring their work-bags of various skins, artistically made and trimmed. These contain moccasins and other garments for their dolls, on which they love to occupy themselves.

The brightly-painted rawhide boxes are reserved for food, and in these the girls bring various prepared meats and other delicacies. This is perhaps the most agreeable part of the play to the chaperon, who is treated as an honored guest at the feast!

Winona seldom plays with boys, even her own brothers and cousins, and after she reaches twelve or fourteen years of age she scarcely speaks to them. Modesty is a virtue which is deeply impressed upon her from early childhood, and the bashfully drooping head, the averted look, the voice low and seldom heard, these are graces much esteemed in a maiden.

She is taught to pay great attention to the care of her long, glossy locks, combing, plaiting, and perfuming them with sweet-scented leaves steeped in oil. Her personal appearance is well understood to be a matter of real moment, and rich dress and ornaments are highly prized. Fortunately they never go out of fashion, and once owned are permanent possessions, unless parted with as ceremonial gifts on some great occasion of mourning or festivity.

When she reaches a marriageable age her father allows her to give a feast to all the other girls of her immediate clan, and this "Feast of Virgins" may only be attended by those of spotless reputation. To have given or attended a number of them is regarded as a choice honor.

Tatiyopa, by the time she is fifteen, has already a name for skill in needlework, and generosity in distributing the articles of her own making. She is now generally called Winona—the charitable and kind! She believes that it is woman's work to make and keep a home that will be worthy of the bravest, and hospitable to all, and in this simple faith she enters upon the realities of her womanhood.

II
WINONA, THE CHILD-WOMAN

Braver than the bravest,
You sought honors at death's door;
Could you not remember
One who weeps at home—
Could you not remember me?

Braver than the bravest,
You sought honors more than love;
Dear, I weep, yet I am not a coward;
My heart weeps for thee—
My heart weeps when I remember thee!
—Sioux Love Song.

The sky is blue overhead, peeping through window-like openings in a roof of green leaves. Right between a great pine and a birch tree their soft doeskin shawls are spread, and there sit two Sioux maidens amid their fineries—variously colored porcupine quills for embroidery laid upon sheets of thin birch-bark, and moccasin tops worked in colors like autumn leaves. It is Winona and her friend Miniyata.

They have arrived at the period during which the young girl is carefully secluded from her brothers and cousins and future lovers, and retires, as it were, into the nunnery of the woods, behind a veil of thick foliage. Thus she is expected to develop fully her womanly qualities. In meditation and solitude, entirely alone or with a chosen companion of her own sex and age, she gains a secret strength, as she studies the art of womanhood from nature herself.

Winona has the robust beauty of the wild lily of the prairie, pure and strong in her deep colors of yellow and scarlet against the savage plain and horizon, basking in the open sun like a child, yet soft and woman-like, with drooping head when observed. Both girls are beautifully robed in loose gowns of soft doeskin, girded about the waist with the usual very wide leather belt.

"Come, let us practice our sacred dance," says one to the other. Each crowns her glossy head with a wreath of wild flowers, and they dance with slow steps around the white birch, singing meanwhile the sacred songs.

Now upon the lake that stretches blue to the eastward there appears a distant canoe, a mere speck, no bigger than a bird far off against the shining sky.

"See the lifting of the paddles!" exclaims Winona.

"Like the leaping of a trout upon the water!" suggests Miniyata.

"I hope they will not discover us, yet I would like to know who they are," remarks the other, innocently.

The birch canoe approaches swiftly, with two young men plying the light cedar paddles.

The girls now settle down to their needlework, quite as if they had never laughed or danced or woven garlands, bending over their embroidery in perfect silence. Surely they would not wish to attract attention, for the two sturdy young warriors have already landed.

They pick up the canoe and lay it well up on the bank, out of sight. Then one procures a strong pole. They lift a buck deer from the canoe—not a mark upon it, save for the bullet wound; the deer looks as if it were sleeping! They tie the hind legs together and the fore legs also and carry it between them on the pole.

Quickly and cleverly they do all this; and now they start forward and come unexpectedly upon the maidens' retreat! They pause for an instant in mute apology, but the girls smile their forgiveness, and the youths hurry on toward the village.

Winona has now attended her first maidens' feast and is considered eligible to marriage. She may receive young men, but not in public or in a social way, for such was not the custom of the Sioux. When he speaks, she need not answer him unless she chooses.

The Indian woman in her quiet way preserves the dignity of the home. From our standpoint the white man is a law-breaker! The "Great Mystery," we say, does not adorn the woman above the man. His law is spreading horns, or flowing mane, or gorgeous plumage for the male; the female he made plain, but comely, modest and gentle. She is the foundation of man's dignity and honor. Upon her rests the life of the home and of the family. I have often thought that there is much in this philosophy of an untutored people. Had her husband remained long enough in one place, the Indian woman, I believe, would have developed no mean civilization and culture of her own.

It was no disgrace to the chief's daughter in the old days to work with her hands. Indeed, their standard of worth was the willingness to work, but not for the sake of accumulation, only in order to give. Winona has learned to prepare skins, to remove the hair and tan the skin of a deer so that it may be made into moccasins within three days. She has a bone tool for each stage of the conversion of the stiff raw-hide into velvety leather. She has been taught the art of painting tents and raw-hide cases, and the manufacture of garments of all kinds.

Generosity is a trait that is highly developed in the Sioux woman. She makes many moccasins and other articles of clothing for her male relatives, or for any who are not well provided. She loves to see her brother the best dressed among the young men, and the moccasins especially of a young brave are the pride of his woman-kind.

Her own person is neatly attired, but ordinarily with great simplicity. Her doeskin gown has wide, flowing sleeves; the neck is low, but not so low as is the evening dress of society.

Her moccasins are plain; her leggins close-fitting and not as high as her brother's. She parts her smooth, jet-black hair in the middle and plaits it in two. In the old days she used to do it in one plait wound around with wampum. Her ornaments, sparingly worn, are beads, elks' teeth, and a touch of red paint. No feathers are worn by the woman, unless in a sacred dance.

She is supposed to be always occupied with some feminine pursuit or engaged in some social affair, which also is strictly feminine as a rule. Even her language is peculiar to her sex, some words being used by women only, while others have a feminine termination.

There is an etiquette of sitting and standing, which is strictly observed. The woman must never raise her knees or cross her feet when seated. She seats herself on the ground sidewise, with both feet under her.

Notwithstanding her modesty and undemonstrative ways, there is no lack of mirth and relaxation for Winona among her girl companions.

In summer, swimming and playing in the water is a favorite amusement. She even imitates with the soles of her feet the peculiar, resonant sound that the beaver makes with her large, flat tail upon the surface of the water. She is a graceful swimmer, keeping the feet together and waving them backward and forward like the tail of a fish.

Nearly all her games are different from those of the men. She has a sport of wand-throwing which develops fine muscles of the shoulder and back. The wands are about eight feet long, and taper gradually from an inch and a half to half an inch in diameter. Some of them are artistically made, with heads of bone and horn, so that it is remarkable to what a distance they may be made to slide over the ground. In the feminine game of ball, which is something like "shinny," the ball is driven with curved sticks between two goals. It is played with from two or three to a hundred on a side, and a game between two bands or villages is a picturesque event.

A common indoor diversion is the "deer's foot" game, played with six deer hoofs on a string, ending in a bone or steel awl. The object is to throw it in such a way as to catch one or more hoofs on the point of the awl, a feat which requires no little dexterity. Another is played with marked plum-stones in a bowl, which are thrown like dice and count according to the side that is turned uppermost.

Winona's wooing is a typical one. As with any other people, love-making is more or less in vogue at all times of the year, but more especially at midsummer, during the characteristic reunions and festivities of that season. The young men go about usually in pairs, and the maidens do likewise. They may meet by chance at any time of day, in the woods or at the spring, but oftenest seek to do so after dark, just outside the teepee. The girl has her companion, and he has his, for the sake of propriety or protection. The conversation is carried on in a whisper, so that even these chaperons do not hear.

At the sound of the drum on summer evenings, dances are begun within the circular rows of teepees, but without the circle the young men promenade in pairs. Each provides himself with the plaintive flute and plays the simple cadences of his people, while his person is completely covered with his fine robe, so that he cannot be recognized by the passerby. At every pause in the melody he gives his yodel-like love-call, to which the girls respond with their musical, sing-song laughter.

Matosapa has loved Winona since the time he saw her at the lakeside in her parlor among the pines. But he has not had much opportunity to speak until on such a night, after the dances are over. There is no outside fire; but a dim light from within the skin teepees sheds a mellow glow over the camp, mingling with the light of a young moon. Thus these lovers go about like ghosts. Matosapa has already circled the teepees with his inseparable brother-friend, Brave Elk.

"Friend, do me an honor to-night!" he exclaims, at last. "Open this first door for me, since this will be the first time I shall speak to a woman!"

"Ah," suggests Brave Elk, "I hope you have selected a girl whose grandmother has no cross dogs!"

"The prize that is won at great risk is usually valued most," replies Matosapa.

"Ho, kola! I shall touch the door-flap as softly as the swallow alights upon her nest. But I warn you, do not let your heart beat too loudly, for the old woman's ears are still good!"

So, joking and laughing, they proceed toward a large buffalo tent with a horse's tail suspended from the highest pole to indicate the rank of the owner. They have ceased to blow the flute some paces back, and walk noiselessly as a panther in quest of a doe.

Brave Elk opens the door. Matosapa enters the tent. As was the wont of the Sioux, the well-born maid has a little teepee within a teepee—a private apartment of her own. He passes the sleeping family to this inner shrine. There he gently wakens Winona with proper apologies. This is not unusual or strange to her innocence, for it was the custom of the people. He sits at the door, while his friend waits outside, and tells his love in a whisper. To this she does not reply at once; even if she loves him, it is proper that she should be silent. The lover does not know whether he is favorably received or not, upon this his first visit. He must now seek her outside upon every favorable occasion. No gifts are offered at this stage of the affair; the trafficking in ponies and "buying" a wife is entirely a modern custom.

Matosapa has improved every opportunity, until Winona has at last shyly admitted her willingness to listen. For a whole year he has been compelled at intervals to repeat the story of his love. Through the autumn hunting of the buffalo and the long, cold winter he often presents her kinsfolk with his game.

At the next midsummer the parents on both sides are made acquainted with the betrothal, and they at once begin preparations for the coming wedding. Provisions and delicacies of all kinds are laid aside for a feast. Matosapa's sisters and his girl cousins are told of the approaching event, and they too prepare for it, since it is their duty to dress or adorn the bride with garments made by their own hands.

With the Sioux of the old days, the great natural crises of human life, marriage and birth, were considered sacred and hedged about with great privacy. Therefore the union is publicly celebrated after and not before its consummation. Suddenly the young couple disappear. They go out into the wilderness together, and spend some days or weeks away from the camp. This is their honeymoon, away from all curious or prying eyes. In due time they quietly return, he to his home and she to hers, and now at last the marriage is announced and invitations are given to the feast.

The bride is ceremoniously delivered to her husband's people, together with presents of rich clothing collected from all her clan, which she afterward distributes among her new relations. Winona is carried in a travois handsomely decorated, and is received with equal ceremony. For several days following she is dressed and painted by the female relatives of the groom, each in her turn, while in both clans the wedding feast is celebrated.

To illustrate womanly nobility of nature, let me tell the story of Dowanhotaninwin, Her-Singing-Heard. The maiden was deprived of both father and mother when scarcely ten years old, by an attack of the Sacs and Foxes while they were on a hunting expedition. Left alone with her grandmother, she was carefully reared and trained by this sage of the wild life.

Nature had given her more than her share of attractiveness, and she was womanly and winning as she was handsome. Yet she remained unmarried for nearly thirty years—a most unusual thing among us; and although she had worthy suitors in every branch of the Sioux nation, she quietly refused every offer.

Certain warriors who had distinguished themselves against the particular tribe who had made her an orphan, persistently sought her hand in marriage, but failed utterly.

One summer the Sioux and the Sacs and Foxes were brought together under a flag of truce by the Commissioners of the Great White Father, for the purpose of making a treaty with them. During the short period of friendly intercourse and social dance and feast, a noble warrior of the enemy's tribe courted Dowanhotaninwin.

Several of her old lovers were vying with one another to win her at the same time, that she might have inter-tribal celebration of her wedding.

Behold! the maiden accepted the foe of her childhood—one of those who had cruelly deprived her of her parents!

By night she fled to the Sac and Fox camp with her lover. It seemed at first an insult to the Sioux, and there was almost an outbreak among the young men of the tribe, who were barely restrained by their respect for the Commissioners of the Great Father.

But her aged grandfather explained the matter publicly in this fashion:

"Young men, hear ye! Your hearts are strong; let them not be troubled by the act of a young woman of your tribe! This has been her secret wish since she became a woman. She deprecates all tribal warfare. Her young heart never forgot its early sorrow; yet she has never blamed the Sacs and Foxes or held them responsible for the deed. She blames rather the customs of war among us. She believes in the formation of a blood brotherhood strong enough to prevent all this cruel and useless enmity. This was her high purpose, and to this end she reserved her hand. Forgive her, forgive her, I pray!"

In the morning there was a great commotion. The herald of the Sacs and Foxes entered the Sioux camp, attired in ceremonial garb and bearing in one hand an American flag and in the other a peace-pipe. He made the rounds singing a peace song, and delivering to all an invitation to attend the wedding feast of Dowanhotaninwin and their chief's son. Thus all was well. The simplicity, high purpose, and bravery of the girl won the hearts of the two tribes, and as long as she lived she was able to keep the peace between them.

III
SNANA'S FAWN

The Little Missouri was in her spring fullness, and the hills among which she found her way to the Great Muddy were profusely adorned with colors, much like those worn by the wild red man upon a holiday! Looking toward the sunrise, one saw mysterious, deep shadows and bright prominences, while on the opposite side there was really an extravagant array of variegated hues. Between the gorgeous buttes and rainbow-tinted ridges there were narrow plains, broken here and there by dry creeks or gulches, and these again were clothed scantily with poplars and sad-colored bull-berry bushes, while the bare spots were purple with the wild Dakota crocuses.

Upon the lowest of a series of natural terraces there stood on this May morning a young Sioux girl, whose graceful movements were not unlike those of a doe which chanced to be lurking in a neighboring gulch. On the upper plains, not far away, were her young companions, all busily employed with the wewoptay, as it was called—the sharp-pointed stick with which the Sioux women dig wild turnips. They were gayly gossiping together, or each humming a love-song as she worked, only Snana stood somewhat apart from the rest; in fact, concealed by the crest of the ridge.

She had paused in her digging and stood facing the sun-kissed buttes. Above them in the clear blue sky the father sun was traveling upward as in haste, while to her receptive spirit there appealed an awful, unknown force, the silent speech of the Great Mystery, to which it seemed to her the whole world must be listening!

"O Great Mystery! the father of earthly things is coming to quicken us into life. Have pity on me, I pray thee! May I some day become the mother of a great and brave race of warriors!" So the maiden prayed silently.

It was now full-born day. The sun shone hot upon the bare ground, and the drops stood upon Snana's forehead as she plied her long pole. There was a cool spring in the dry creek bed near by, well hidden by a clump of chokecherry bushes, and she turned thither to cool her thirsty throat. In the depths of the ravine her eye caught a familiar footprint—the track of a doe with the young fawn beside it. The hunting instinct arose within.

"It will be a great feat if I can find and take from her the babe. The little tawny skin shall be beautifully dressed by my mother. The legs and the nose shall be embossed with porcupine quills. It will be my work-bag," she said to herself.

As she stole forward on the fresh trail she scanned every nook, every clump of bushes. There was a sudden rustle from within a grove of wild plum trees, thickly festooned with grape and clematis, and the doe mother bounded away as carelessly as if she were never to return.

Ah, a mother's ruse! Snana entered the thorny enclosure, which was almost a rude teepee, and, tucked away in the furthermost corner, lay something with a trout-like, speckled, tawny coat. She bent over it. The fawn was apparently sleeping. Presently its eyes moved a bit, and a shiver passed through its subtle body.

"Thou shalt not die; thy skin shall not become my work-bag!" unconsciously the maiden spoke. The mother sympathy had taken hold on her mind. She picked the fawn up tenderly, bound its legs, and put it on her back to carry like an Indian babe in the folds of her robe.

"I cannot leave you alone, Tachinchala. Your mother is not here. Our hunters will soon return by this road, and your mother has left behind her two plain tracks leading to this thicket," she murmured.

The wild creature struggled vigorously for a minute, and then became quiet. Its graceful head protruded from the elkskin robe just over Snana's shoulder. She was slowly climbing the slope with her burden, when suddenly like an apparition the doe-mother stood before her. The fawn called loudly when it was first seized, and the mother was not too far away to hear. Now she called frantically for her child, at the same time stamping with her delicate fore-feet.

"Yes, sister, you are right; she is yours; but you cannot save her to-day! The hunters will soon be here. Let me keep her for you; I will return her to you safely. And hear me, O sister of the woods, that some day I may become the mother of a noble race of warriors and of fine women, as handsome as you are!"

At this moment the quick eyes of the Indian girl detected something strange in the doe's actions. She glanced in every direction and behold! a grizzly bear was cautiously approaching the group from a considerable distance.

"Run, run, sister! I shall save your child if I can," she cried, and flew for the nearest scrub oak on the edge of the bank. Up the tree she scrambled, with the fawn still securely bound to her back. The grizzly came on with teeth exposed, and the doe-mother in her flight came between him and the tree, giving a series of indignant snorts as she ran, and so distracted Mato from his object of attack; but only for a few seconds—then on he came!

"Desist, O brave Mato! It does not become a great medicine-man to attack a helpless woman with a burden upon her back!"

Snana spoke as if the huge brute could understand her, and indeed the Indians hold that wild animals understand intuitively when appealed to by human beings in distress. Yet he replied only with a hoarse growl, as rising upon his hind legs he shook the little tree vigorously.

"Ye, ye, heyupi ye!" Snana called loudly to her companion turnip-diggers. Her cry soon brought all the women into sight upon a near-by ridge, and they immediately gave a general alarm. Mato saw them, but appeared not at all concerned and was still intent upon dislodging the girl, who clung frantically to her perch.

Presently there appeared upon the little knoll several warriors, mounted and uttering the usual war-whoop, as if they were about to swoop down upon a human enemy. This touched the dignity of Mato, and he immediately prepared to accept the challenge. Every Indian was alive to the possibilities of the occasion, for it is well known that Mato, or grizzly bear, alone among animals is given the rank of a warrior, so that whoever conquers him may wear an eagle feather.

"Woo! woo!" the warriors shouted, as they maneuvered to draw him into the open plain.

He answered with hoarse growls, threatening a rider who had ventured too near. But arrows were many and well-aimed, and in a few minutes the great and warlike Mato lay dead at the foot of the tree.

The men ran forward and counted their coups on him, just as when an enemy is fallen. Then they looked at one another and placed their hands over their mouths as the young girl descended the tree with a fawn bound upon her back.

"So that was the bait!" they cried. "And will you not make a feast with that fawn for us who came to your rescue?"

"The fawn is young and tender, and we have not eaten meat for two days. It will be a generous thing to do," added her father, who was among them.

"Ye-e-e!" she cried out in distress. "Do not ask it! I have seen this fawn's mother. I have promised to keep her child safe. See! I have saved its life, even when my own was in danger."

"Ho, ho, wakan ye lo! (Yes, yes, 'tis holy or mysterious)," they exclaimed approvingly.

It was no small trouble for Snana to keep her trust. As may well be supposed, all the dogs of the teepee village must be watched and kept at a distance. Neither was it easy to feed the little captive; but in gaining its confidence the girl was an adept. The fawn soon followed her everywhere, and called to her when hungry exactly as she had called to her own mother.

After several days, when her fright at the encounter with the bear had somewhat worn off, Snana took her pet into the woods and back to the very spot in which she had found it. In the furthest corner of the wild plum grove she laid it down, gently stroked its soft forehead, and smoothed the leaflike ears. The little thing closed its eyes. Once more the Sioux girl bent over and laid her cheek against the fawn's head; then reluctantly she moved away, hoping and yet dreading that the mother would return. She crouched under a clump of bushes near by, and gave the doe call. It was a reckless thing for her to do, for such a call might bring upon her a mountain lion or ever-watchful silvertip; but Snana did not think of that.

In a few minutes she heard the light patter of hoofs, and caught a glimpse of a doe running straight toward the fawn's hiding-place. When she stole near enough to see, the doe and the fawn were examining one another carefully, as if fearing some treachery. At last both were apparently satisfied. The doe caressed her natural child, and the little one accepted the milk she offered.

In the Sioux maiden's mind there was turmoil. A close attachment to the little wild creature had already taken root there, contending with the sense of justice that was strong within her. Now womanly sympathy for the mother was in control, and now a desire to possess and protect her helpless pet.

"I can take care of her against all hunters, both animal and human. They are ever ready to seize the helpless fawn for food. Her life will be often exposed. You cannot save her from disaster. O, Takcha, my sister, let me still keep her for you!" she finally appealed to the poor doe, who was nervously watching the intruder, and apparently thinking how she might best escape with the fawn.

Just at this moment there came a low call from the wood. It was a doe call; but the wild mother and her new friend both knew that it was not the call of a real doe.

"It is a Sioux hunter!" whispered the girl. "You must go, my sister! Be off; I will take your child to safety!"

While she was yet speaking, the doe seemed to realize the danger. She stopped only an instant to lick fondly the tawny coat of the little one, who had just finished her dinner; then she bounded away.

As Snana emerged from the bushes with her charge, a young hunter met her face to face, and stared at her curiously. He was not of her father's camp, but a stranger.

"Ugh, you have my game."

"Tosh!" she replied coquettishly.

It was so often said among the Indians that the doe was wont to put on human form to mislead the hunter, that it looked strange to see a woman with a fawn, and the young man could not forbear to gaze upon Snana.

"You are not the real mother in maiden's guise? Tell me truly if you are of human blood," he demanded rudely.

"I am a Sioux maiden! Do you not know my father?" she replied.

"Ah, but who is your father? What is his name?" he insisted, nervously fingering his arrows.

"Do not be a coward! Surely you should know a maid of your own race," she replied reproachfully.

"Ah, you know the tricks of the doe! What is thy name?"

"Hast thou forgotten the etiquette of thy people, and wouldst compel me to pronounce my own name? I refuse; thou art jesting!" she retorted with a smile.

"Thou dost give the tricky answers of a doe. I cannot wait; I must act before I lose my natural mind. But already I am yours. Whatever purpose you may have in thus charming a poor hunter, be merciful," and, throwing aside his quiver, he sat down.

The maiden stole a glance at his face, and then another. He was handsome. Softly she reentered the thicket and laid down the little fawn.

"Promise me never to hunt here again!" she said earnestly, as she came forth without her pretty burden, and he exacted another promise in return. Thus Snana lost her fawn, and found a lover.

IV
SHE-WHO-HAS-A-SOUL

It was a long time ago, nearly two hundred years ago, that some of our people were living upon the shores of the Great Lake, Lake Superior. The chief of this band was called Tatankaota, Many Buffaloes.

One day the young son of Tatankaota led a war-party against the Ojibways, who occupied the country east of us, toward the rising sun.

When they had gone a day's journey in the direction of Sault Ste. Marie, in our language Skesketatanka, the warriors took up their position on the lake shore, at a point which the Ojibways were accustomed to pass in their canoes.

Long they gazed, and scanned the surface of the water, watching for the coming of the foe. The sun had risen above the dark pines, over the great ridge of woodland across the bay. It was the awakening of all living things. The birds were singing, and shining fishes leaped out of the water as if at play. At last, far off, there came the warning cry of the loon to stir their expectant ears.

"Warriors, look close to the horizon! This brother of ours does not lie. The enemy comes!" exclaimed their leader.

Presently upon the sparkling face of the water there appeared a moving canoe. There was but one, and it was coming directly toward them.

"Hahatonwan! Hahatonwan! (The Ojibways! the Ojibways!)" they exclaimed with one voice, and, grasping their weapons, they hastily concealed themselves in the bushes.

"Spare none—take no captives!" ordered the chief's son.

Nearer and nearer approached the strange canoe. The glistening blades of its paddles flashed as it were the signal of good news, or a welcome challenge. All impatiently waited until it should come within arrow-shot.

"Surely it is an Ojibway canoe," one murmured. "Yet look! the stroke is ungainly!" Now, among all the tribes only the Ojibway's art is perfect in paddling a birch canoe. This was a powerful stroke, but harsh and unsteady.

"See! there are no feathers on this man's head!" exclaimed the son of the chief. "Hold, warriors, he wears a woman's dress, and I see no weapon. No courage is needed to take his life, therefore let it be spared! I command that only coups (or blows) be counted on him, and he shall tell us whence he comes, and on what errand."

The signal was given; the warriors sprang to their feet, and like wolves they sped from the forest, out upon the white, sandy beach and straight into the sparkling waters of the lake, giving the shrill war-cry, the warning of death!

The solitary oarsman made no outcry—he offered no defense! Kneeling calmly in the prow of the little vessel, he merely ceased paddling and seemed to await with patience the deadly blow of the tomahawk.

The son of Tatankaota was foremost in the charge, but suddenly an impulse seized him to stop his warriors, lest one in the heat of excitement should do a mischief to the stranger. The canoe with its occupant was now very near, and it could be seen that the expression of his face was very gentle and even benignant. None could doubt his utter harmlessness; and the chief's son afterward declared that at this moment he felt a premonition of some event, but whether good or evil he could not tell.

No blows were struck—no coups counted. The young man bade his warriors take up the canoe and carry it to the shore; and although they murmured somewhat among themselves, they did as he commanded them. They seized the light bark and bore it dripping to a hill covered with tall pines, and overlooking the waters of the Great Lake.

Then the warriors lifted their war-clubs over their heads and sang, standing around the canoe in which the black-robed stranger was still kneeling. Looking at him closely, they perceived that he was of a peculiar complexion, pale and inclined to red. He wore a necklace of beads, from which hung a cross bearing the form of a man. His garments were strange, and most like the robes of woman. All of these things perplexed them greatly.

Presently the Black Robe told them by signs, in response to their inquiries, that he came from the rising sun, even beyond the Great Salt Water, and he seemed to say that he formerly came from the sky. Upon this the warriors believed that he must be a prophet or mysterious man.

Their leader directed them to take up again the canoe with the man in it, and appointed the warriors to carry it by turns until they should reach his father's village. This was done according to the ancient custom, as a mark of respect and honor. They took it up forthwith, and traveled with all convenient speed along the lake shore, through forests and across streams to a place called the Maiden's Retreat, a short distance from the village.

Thence the chief's son sent a messenger to announce to his father that he was bringing home a stranger, and to ask whether or not he should be allowed to enter the village. "His appearance," declared the scout, "is unlike that of any man we have ever seen, and his ways are mysterious!"

When the chief heard these words, he immediately called his council-men together to decide what was to be done, for he feared by admitting the mysterious stranger to bring some disaster upon his people. Finally he went out with his wisest men to meet his son's war-party. They looked with astonishment upon the Black Robe.

"Dispatch him! Dispatch him! Show him no mercy!" cried some of the council-men.

"Let him go on his way unharmed. Trouble him not," advised others.

"It is well known that the evil spirits sometimes take the form of a man or animal. From his strange appearance I judge this to be such a one. He should be put to death, lest some harm befall our people," an old man urged.

By this time several of the women of the village had reached the spot. Among them was She-who-has-a-Soul, the chief's youngest daughter, who tradition says was a maiden of much beauty, and of a generous heart. The stranger was evidently footsore from much travel and

weakened by fasting. When she saw that the poor man clasped his hands and looked skyward as he uttered words in an unknown tongue, she pleaded with her father that a stranger who has entered their midst unchallenged may claim the hospitality of the people, according to the ancient custom.

"Father, he is weary and in want of food. Hold him no longer! Delay your council until he is refreshed!" These were the words of She-who-has-a-Soul, and her father could not refuse her prayer. The Black Robe was released, and the Sioux maiden led him to her father's teepee.

Now the warriors had been surprised and indeed displeased to find him dressed after the fashion of a woman, and they looked upon him with suspicion. But from the moment that she first beheld him, the heart of the maiden had turned toward this strange and seemingly unfortunate man. It appeared to her that great reverence and meekness were in his face, and with it all she was struck by his utter fearlessness, his apparent unconsciousness of danger.

The chief's daughter, having gained her father's permission, invited the Black Robe to his great buffalo-skin tent, and spreading a fine robe, she gently asked him to be seated. With the aid of her mother, she prepared wild rice sweetened with maple sugar and some broiled venison for his repast. The youthful warriors were astonished to observe these attentions, but the maiden heeded them not. She anointed the blistered feet of the holy man with perfumed otter oil, and put upon him a pair of moccasins beautifully worked by her own hands.

It was only an act of charity on her part, but the young men were displeased, and again urged that the stranger should at once be turned away. Some even suggested harsher measures; but they were overruled by the chief, softened by the persuasions of a well-beloved daughter.

During the few days that the Black Robe remained in the Sioux village he preached earnestly to the maiden, for she had been permitted to converse with him by signs, that she might try to ascertain what manner of man he was. He told her of the coming of a "Great Prophet" from the sky, and of his words that he had left with the people. The cross with the figure of a man he explained as his totem which he had told them to carry. He also said that those who love him are commanded to go among strange peoples to tell the news, and that all who believe must be marked with holy water and accept the totem.

He asked by signs if She-who-has-a-Soul believed the story. To this she replied:

"It is a sweet story—a likely legend! I do believe!"

Then the good father took out a small cross, and having pressed it to his heart and crossed his forehead and breast, he gave it to her. Finally he dipped his finger in water and touched the forehead of the maiden, repeating meanwhile some words in an unknown tongue.

The mother was troubled, for she feared that the stranger was trying to bewitch her daughter, but the chief decided thus:

"This is a praying-man, and he is not of our people; his customs are different, but they are not evil. Warriors, take him back to the spot where you saw him first! It is my desire, and the good custom of our tribe requires that you free him without injury!"

Accordingly they formed a large party, and carried the Black Robe in his canoe back to the shore of the Great Lake, to the place where they had met him, and he was allowed to depart thence whithersoever he would. He took his leave with signs of gratitude for their hospitality, and especially for the kindness of the beautiful Sioux maiden. She seemed to have understood his mission better than any one else, and as long as she lived she kept his queer trinket—as it seemed to the others—and performed the strange acts that he had taught her.

Furthermore, it was through the pleadings of She-who-has-a-Soul that the chief Tatankaota advised his people in after days to befriend the white strangers, and though many of the other chiefs opposed him in this, his counsels prevailed. Hence it was that both the French and English received much kindness from our people, mainly through the influence of this one woman!

Such was the first coming of the white man among us, as it is told in our traditions. Other praying-men came later, and many of the Sioux allowed themselves to be baptized. True, there have been Indian wars, but not without reason; and it is pleasant to remember that the Sioux were hospitable to the first white "prayingman," and that it was a tender-hearted maiden of my people who first took in her hands the cross of the new religion.

V
THE PEACE-MAKER

One of the most remarkable women of her day and nation was Eyatonkawee, She-whose-Voice-is-heard-afar. It is matter of history among the Wakpaykootay band of Sioux, the Dwellers among the Leaves, that when Eyatonkawee was a very young woman she was once victorious in a hand-to-hand combat with the enemy in the woods of Minnesota, where her people were hunting the deer. At such times they often met with stray parties of Sacs and Foxes from the prairies of Iowa and Illinois.

Now, the custom was among our people that the doer of a notable warlike deed was held in highest honor, and these deeds were kept constantly in memory by being recited in public, before many witnesses. The greatest exploit was that one involving most personal courage and physical address, and he whose record was adjudged best might claim certain privileges, not the least of which was the right to interfere in any quarrel and separate the combatants. The peace-maker might resort to force, if need be, and no one dared to utter a protest who could not say that he had himself achieved an equal fame.

There was a man called Tamahay, known to Minnesota history as the "One-eyed Sioux," who was a notable character on the frontier in the early part of the nineteenth century. He was very reckless, and could boast of many a perilous adventure. He was the only Sioux who, in the War of 1812, fought for the Americans, while all the rest of his people sided with the British, mainly through the influence of the English traders among them at that time. This same "One-eyed Sioux" became a warm friend of Lieutenant Pike, who discovered the sources of the Mississippi, and for whom Pike's Peak is named. Some say that the Indian took his friend's name, for Tamahay in English means Pike or Pickerel.

Unfortunately, in later life this brave man became a drunkard, and after the Americans took possession of his country almost any one of them would supply him with liquor in recognition of his notable services as a scout and soldier. Thus he was at times no less dangerous in camp than in battle.

Now, Eyatonkawee, being a young widow, had married the son of a lesser chief in Tamahay's band, and was living among strangers. Moreover, she was yet young and modest.

One day this bashful matron heard loud warwhoops and the screams of women. Looking forth, she saw the people fleeing hither and thither, while Tamahay, half intoxicated, rushed from his teepee painted for war, armed with tomahawk and scalping-knife, and approached another warrior as if to slay him. At this sight her heart became strong, and she quickly sprang between them with her woman's knife in her hand.

"It was a Sac warrior of like proportions and bravery with your own, who, having slain several of the Sioux, thus approached me with uplifted tomahawk!" she exclaimed in a clear voice, and went on to recite her victory on that famous day so that the terrified people paused to hear.

Tamahay was greatly astonished, but he was not too drunk to realize that he must give way at once, or be subject to the humiliation of a blow from the woman-warrior who challenged him thus. The whole camp was listening; and being unable, in spite of his giant frame and well-known record, to cite a greater deed than hers, he retreated with as good a grace as possible. Thus Eyatonkawee recounted her brave deed for the first time, in order to save a man's life. From that day her name was great as a peace-maker—greater even than when she had first defended so gallantly her babe and home!

Many years afterward, when she had attained middle age, this woman averted a serious danger from her people.

Chief Little Crow the elder was dead, and as he had two wives of two different bands, the succession was disputed among the half-brothers and their adherents. Finally the two sons of the wife belonging to the Wabashaw band plotted against the son of the woman of the Kaposia band, His-Red-Nation by name, afterward called Little Crow—the man who led the Minnesota massacre.

They obtained a quantity of whisky and made a great feast to which many were invited, intending when all were more or less intoxicated to precipitate a fight in which he should be killed. It would be easy afterward to excuse themselves by saying that it was an accident.

Mendota, near what is now the thriving city of Saint Paul, then a queen of trading-posts in the Northwest, was the rendezvous of the Sioux. The event brought many together, for all warriors of note were bidden from far and near, and even the great traders of the day were present, for the succession to the chieftainship was one which vitally affected their interests.

During the early part of the day all went well, with speeches and eulogies of the dead chief, flowing and eloquent, such as only a native orator can utter. Presently two goodly kegs of whisky were rolled into the council teepee.

Eyatonkawee was among the women, and heard their expressions of anxiety as the voices of the men rose louder and more threatening. Some carried their children away into the woods for safety, while others sought speech with their husbands outside the council lodge and besought them to come away in time. But more than this was needed to cope with the emergency. Suddenly a familiar form appeared in the door of the council lodge.

"Is it becoming in a warrior to spill the blood of his tribesmen? Are there no longer any Ojibways?"

It was the voice of Eyatonkawee, that stronghearted woman! Advancing at the critical moment to the middle of the ring of warriors, she once more recited her "brave deed" with all the accompaniment of action and gesture, and to such effect that the disorderly feast broke up in confusion, and there was peace between the rival bands of Sioux.

There was seldom a dangerous quarrel among the Indians in those days that was not precipitated by the use of strong liquor, and this simple Indian woman, whose good judgment was equal to her courage, fully recognized this fact. All her life, and especially after her favorite brother had been killed in a drunken brawl in the early days of the American Fur Company, she was a determined enemy to strong drink, and it is said did more to prevent its use among her immediate band than any other person. Being a woman, her sole means of recognition was the "brave deed" which she so wonderfully described and enacted before the people.

During the lifetime of She-whose-Voice-is-heard-afar—and she died only a few years ago—it behooved the Sioux men, if they drank at all, to drink secretly and in moderation. There are many who remember her brave entrance upon the scene of carousal, and her dramatic recital of the immortal deed of her youth.

"Hanta! hanta wo! (Out of the way!)" exclaim the dismayed warriors, scrambling in every direction to avoid the upraised arm of the terrible old woman, who bursts suddenly upon them with disheveled hair, her gown torn and streaked here and there with what looks like fresh blood, her leather leggins loose and ungartered, as if newly come from the famous struggle. One of the men has a keg of whisky for which he has given a pony, and the others have been invited in for a night of pleasure. But scarcely has the first round been drunk to the toast of "great deeds," when Eyatonkawee is upon them, her great knife held high in her wrinkled left hand, her tomahawk in the right. Her black eyes gleam as she declaims in a voice strong, unterrified:

"Look! look! brothers and husbands—the Sacs and Foxes are upon us!

Behold, our braves are surprised—they are unprepared!

Hear the mothers, the wives and the children screaming in affright!

"Your brave sister, Eyatonkawee, she, the newly made mother,

is serving the smoking venison to her husband, just returned from the chase!

Ah, he plunges into the thickest of the enemy!

He falls, he falls, in full view of his young wife!

"She desperately presses her babe to her breast,

while on they come yelling and triumphant!

The foremost of them all enters her white buffalo-skin teepee:

Tossing her babe at the warrior's feet, she stands before him, defiant;

But he straightway levels his spear at her bosom.

Quickly she springs aside, and as quickly deals a deadly blow with her ax:

Falls at her feet the mighty warrior!

"Closely following on comes another,

unknowing what fate has met his fellow!

He too enters her teepee, and upon his feather-decked head her ax falls —Only his death-groan replies!

"Another of heroic size and great prowess,

as witnessed by his war-bonnet of eagle-feathers,

Rushes on, yelling and whooping—for they believe

that victory is with them!

The third great warrior who has dared to enter Eyatonkawee's teepee uninvited, he has already dispatched her husband!

He it is whose terrible war-cry has scattered her sisters among the trees of the forest!

"On he comes with confidence and a brave heart,
seeking one more bloody deed-
One more feather to win for his head!
Behold, he lifts above her woman's head his battle-ax!
No hope, no chance for her life!...
Ah! he strikes beyond her—only the handle of the ax falls heavily upon her tired shoulder!

Her ready knife finds his wicked heart,—
Down he falls at her feet!

"Now the din of war grows fainter and further.

The Sioux recover heart, and drive the enemy headlong from their lodges:

Your sister stands victorious over three!

"She takes her baby boy, and makes him count with his tiny hands the first 'coup' on each dead hero;

Hence he wears the 'first feathers' while yet in his oaken cradle.

"The bravest of the whole Sioux nation have given the war-whoop in your sister's honor, and have said:

'Tis Eyatonkawee who is not satisfied with downing the mighty oaks with her ax—

She took the mighty Sacs and Foxes for trees,
and she felled them with a will!'"

In such fashion the old woman was wont to chant her story, and not a warrior there could tell one to surpass it! The custom was strong, and there was not one to prevent her when she struck open with a single blow of her ax the keg of whisky, and the precious liquor trickled upon the ground.

"So trickles under the ax of Eyatonkawee the blood of an enemy to the Sioux!"

VI
BLUE SKY

Many years ago a large body of the Sioux were encamped at midsummer in the valley of the Cheyenne. It was customary at that period for the Indians to tie up their ponies over night within the circle of the teepees, whenever they were in disputed territory, for they considered it no wrong to steal the horses of the enemy. Hence this long procession of young men and maidens, returning at sunset to the camp with great bundles of green grass hanging gracefully from their saddles!

The "green grass parade" became a regular custom, and in fact a full-dress affair, since it was found to afford unusual opportunities for courtship.

Blue Sky, the pretty daughter of the Sioux chief, put on her best doeskin gown trimmed with elks' teeth, and investing her favorite spotted pony with his beaded saddle-blanket, she went forth in company with one of her maiden friends. Soon two young warriors overtook the pair; and as they approached they covered their heads with their robes, exposing only the upper part of the face disguised with paint and the single eagle feather standing upright. One carried a bow and quiver full of arrows; the other, a war-club suspended from his right arm.

"Ah, hay, hun, hay!" saluted one of them; but the modest maidens said never a word! It was not their way to speak; only the gay calico ponies pranced about and sportively threw back their ears to snap at the horses of the two young men.

"'Tis a brave welcome your horses are giving us!" he continued, while the two girls merely looked at one another with perfect understanding.

Presently Matoska urged his pony close to the Blue Sky's side.

"It may be that I am overbold," he murmured in her ear, "to repeat so soon my tale of love! I know well that I risk a reprimand, if not in words, then by a look or action!"

He paused to note the effect of his speech; but alas! it is the hard rule of savage courtship that the maiden may with propriety and dignity keep silence as long as she wishes, and it is often exasperatingly long.

"I have spoken to no maiden," he resumed, "because I wished to win the war-bonnet before doing so. But to you I was forced to yield!" Again he paused, as if fearing to appear unduly hasty; but deliberate as were speech and manner, his eyes betrayed him. They were full of intense eagerness mingled with anxiety.

"Sometimes I have imagined that I am in the world with you alone, traveling over the prairie of life, or sitting in our lonely white teepee, as the oriole sits with his mate before their swaying home. Yet I seemed to be never lonely, because you were there!" He finished his plea, and with outward calmness awaited her reply.

The maiden had not lost a word, but she was still thinking. She thought that a man is much like the wind of the north, only pleasant and comfortable in midsummer! She feared that she might some time have to furnish all the fuel for their love's fires; therefore she held her peace. Matoska waited for several minutes and then silently withdrew, bearing his disappointment with dignity.

Meanwhile the camp was astir with the returning youths and maidens, their horses' sides fringed with the long meadow grass, singing plaintive serenades around the circular rows of teepees before they broke up for the night.

It was a clear and quiet night; the evening fires were kindled and every teepee transformed into an immense Chinese lantern. There was a glowing ring two miles in circumference, with the wooded river bottom on one side and the vast prairie on the other. The Black Hills loomed up in the distance, and the rapids of the wild Cheyenne sent forth a varying peal of music on the wind. The people enjoyed their evening meal, and in the pauses of their talk and laughter the ponies could be heard munching at the bundles of green grass just outside the teepees.

Suddenly a chorus of yells broke cruelly the peace of the camp, followed by the dashing charge of the Crow Indian horsemen! It was met as bravely and quickly by the Sioux; and in the clear, pale moonlight the dusky warriors fought, with the occasional flash of a firearm, while silent weapons flew thick in the air like dragon-flies at sunset.

The brave mothers, wives, and sisters gave their shrill war-cry to inspire their men, and show the enemy that even the Sioux women cannot be daunted by such a fearful surprise!

When the morning sun sent its golden shafts among the teepees, they saw it through glistening tears—happy tears, they said, because the brave dead had met their end in gallant fight—the very end they craved! And among those who fell that night was Brave Hawk, the handsome brother of the Blue Sky.

In a few days the camp was moved to a point further up the Cheyenne and deeper into the bosom of the hills, leaving behind the decorated grave lodges belonging to the honored dead. A great council teepee was pitched, and here the people met to credit those who had earned them with the honors of the fight, that they might thereafter wear the eagle feathers which they had won.

"The first honor," declared the master of ceremonies, "belongs to Brave Hawk, who fell in the battle! He it was who compelled the Crows to retreat, when he bravely charged upon them and knocked from his horse the Crow chief, their war leader."

"Ho, it is true!" exclaimed the warriors in chorus.

"The second honor," he resumed, "belongs to Matoska, the White Bear!"

"Hun, hun, hay!" interposed another, "it is I, Red Owl, who touched the body of the Crow chief second to Brave Hawk!"

It was a definite challenge.

"The warriors who witnessed the act give the coup to Matoska, friend!" persisted the spokesman.

Red Owl was a brave youth and a close rival of Matoska, both for war honors and for the hand of the prettiest maiden in the tribe. He had hoped to be recognized as one who fought in defense of their homes by the side of Brave Hawk; that would please the Blue Sky, he thought; but the honor was conferred upon his rival!

There was a cloud of suppressed irritation on his dusky face as he sullenly departed to his own tent—an action which displeased the council-men. Matoska had not spoken, and this caused him to appear to the better advantage. The worst of it was that Blue Sky herself had entered the ring with the "orphan steed," as it was called—the war-horse of her dead brother, and had therefore seen and heard everything! Tanagila, or Hummingbird, the beautiful charger, decorated according to custom with the honors won by his master, was led away by the girl amidst resounding war-whoops.

Unable to remain quiet, Red Owl went out into the hills to fast and pray. It was sunset of the next day when he again approached the village, and behind a little ridge came suddenly upon Matoska and the girl standing together. It was the first time that they had met since the "green grass parade," and now only by accident, as the sister of Brave Hawk was in deep mourning. However, the lover had embraced his opportunity, and the maiden had said that she was willing to think of the matter. No more words were spoken.

That very night the council drum was struck three times, followed by the warriors' cheer. Everybody knew what that meant. It was an invitation to the young men to go upon the war-path against the Crows!

Blue Sky was unconsciously startled by this sudden announcement. For the first time in her life she felt a fear that she could not explain. The truth was that she loved, and was not yet fully aware of it. In spite of her fresh grief, she had been inexplicably happy since her last meeting with Matoska, for she had seen in him that which is so beautiful, so compelling in man to the eyes of the woman who loves. He, too, now cherished a real hope, and felt as if he could rush into the thickest of the battle to avenge the brother of his beloved!

In a few days the war-party had reached the Big Horn and sent out advance scouts, who reported a large Crow encampment. Their hundreds of horses covered the flats like a great herd of buffalo, they said. It was immediately decided to attack at daybreak, and on a given signal they dashed impetuously upon the formidable camp. Some stampeded and drove off a number of horses, while the main body plunged into the midst of the Crows.

But the enemy were not easily surprised. They knew well the Sioux tactics, and there was a desperate struggle for supremacy. War-club was raised against war-club, and the death-song of the arrow filled the air! Presently the Sioux were forced to retreat, with the Crows in hot pursuit, like wolves after their prey.

Red Owl and Matoska had been among the foremost in the charge, and now they acted as a rear-guard, bravely defending the retreat of their little army, to the admiration of the enemy. At last a Crow raised his spear against Matoska, who in a flash dismounted him with a stroke of his oaken bow; but alas! the blow snapped the bow-string and left him defenseless. At the same instant his horse uttered a scream and fell, throwing its rider headlong!

There was no one near except Red Owl, who clapped his heels to his pony and joined in the retreat, leaving Matoska behind. He arose, threw down his quiver, and advanced alone to meet the oncoming rush of the Crows!

The Sioux had seen him fall. In a few moments he was surrounded by the enemy, and they saw him no more.

The pursuit was stopped, and they paused upon a hilltop to collect the remnant of their force. Red Owl was the last to come up, and it was observed that he did not look like himself.

"Tell us, what were Matoska's last words?" they asked him.

But he silently dismounted and sent an arrow through his faithful steed, to the astonishment of the warriors. Immediately afterward he took out his knife and stabbed himself to the heart.

"Ah!" they exclaimed, "he could not live to share our humiliation!"

The war-party returned defeated and cast down by this unexpected ending to their adventure, having lost some of their bravest and best men. The camp was instantly thrown into mourning. Many were in heavy grief, but none was more deeply stricken than the maiden called the Blue Sky, the daughter of their chief.

She remained within her teepee and wept in secret, for none knew that she had the right to mourn. Yet she believed that her lover had met with misfortune, but not death. Although his name was announced among those warriors who fell in the field, her own heart assured her that it was not so. "I must go to him," she said to herself. "I must know certainly whether he is still among the living!"

The next evening, while the village was yet in the confusion of great trouble and sorrow, Blue Sky rode out upon her favorite pony as if to take him to water as usual, but none saw her return! She hastened to the spot where she had concealed two sacks of provisions and her extra moccasins and materials for sewing. She had no weapon, save her knife and a small hatchet. She knew the country between the Black Hills and the Big Horn, and knew that it was full of perils for man and much more for woman. Yet by traveling only at night and concealing herself in the daytime she hoped to avoid these dangers, and she rode bravely forth on the trail of the returning warriors.

Her dog, Wapayna, had followed the maiden, and she was not sorry to have so faithful a companion. She cautioned him not to bark at or attack strange animals unless they attacked first, and he seemed to understand the propriety of remaining on guard whenever his mistress was asleep.

She reached the Powder River country in safety, and here she had more than once to pick her way among the buffaloes. These wily animals seemed to realize that she was only a woman and unarmed, so that they scarcely kept out of her path. She also crossed the trails of riders, some of them quite fresh, but was fortunate enough not to meet any of them.

At last the maiden attained the divide between the Tongue and the Big Horn rivers. Her heart beat fast, and the sudden sense of her strange mission almost overwhelmed her. She remembered the only time in her life that the Sioux were upon that river, and so had that bit of friendly welcome from the valley—a recollection of childhood!

It was near morning; the moon had set and for a short time darkness prevailed, but the girl's eyes had by this time become accustomed to the dark. She knew the day was at hand, and with its first beams she was safely tucked into one of those round turns left by the river long ago in changing its bed, now become a little grassy hollow sheltered by steep banks, and hidden by a fringe of trees. Here she picketed her pony, and took her own rest. Not until the afternoon shadows were long did she awake and go forth with determination to seek for the battlefield and for the Crow encampment.

It was not long before she came upon the bodies of fallen horses and men. There was Matoska's white charger, with a Sioux arrow in his side, and she divined the treachery of Red Owl! But he was dead, and his death had atoned for the crime. The body of her lover was nowhere to be found; yet how should they have taken the bravest of the Sioux a captive?

"If he had but one arrow left, he would stand and fight! If his bow-string were broken, he would still welcome death with a strong heart," she thought.

The evening was approaching and the Crow village in plain sight. Blue Sky arranged her hair and dress as well as she could like that of a Crow woman, and with an extra robe she made for herself a bundle that looked as if it held a baby in its many wrappings. The community was still celebrating its recent victory over the Sioux, and the camp was alive with songs and dances. In the darkness she approached unnoticed, and singing in an undertone a Crow lullaby, walked back and forth among the lodges, watching eagerly for any signs of him she sought.

At last she came near to the council lodge. There she beheld his face like an apparition through the dusk and the fire-light! He was sitting within, dressed in the gala costume of a Crow.

"O, he is living! he is living!" thought the brave maiden. "O, what shall I do?" Unconsciously she crept nearer and nearer, until the sharp eyes of an Indian detected the slight difference in her manner and dress, and he at once gave the alarm.

"Wah, wah! Epsaraka! Epsaraka! A Sioux! A Sioux!"

In an instant the whole camp had surrounded the girl, who stood in their midst a prisoner, yet undaunted, for she had seen her lover, and the spirit of her ancestors rose within her.

An interpreter was brought, a man who was half Crow and half Sioux.

"Young and pretty daughter of the Sioux!" exclaimed the chief, "tell us how you came here in our midst undetected, and why!"

"Because," replied the Blue Sky, "your brave warriors have slain my only brother, and captured my lover, whom you now hold a prisoner. It is for his sake that I have thus risked my life and honor!"

"Ho, ho! You are the bravest woman I have ever seen. Your lover was betrayed into our hands by the treachery of one of his own tribe, who shot his horse from behind. He faced us without fear, but it was not his courage that saved his life. He resembles my own son, who lately fell in battle, and according to the custom I have adopted him as my son!"

Thus the brave maiden captured the heart of the wily Crow, and was finally allowed to return home with her lover, bearing many and rich presents. Her name is remembered among the two tribes, for this act of hers resulted in a treaty of peace between them which was kept for a generation.

VII
THE FAITHFULNESS OF LONG EARS

Away beyond the Thin Hills, above the Big Lone Tree upon the Powder River, the Uncpapa Sioux had celebrated their Sun Dance, some forty years ago. It was midsummer and the red folk were happy. They lacked for nothing. The yellowish green flat on either side of the Powder was studded with wild flowers, and the cottonwood trees were in full leaf. One large circle of buffalo skin teepees formed the movable village. The Big Horn Mountains loomed up against the deep blue sky to the westward, and the Black Hills appeared in the far southeast.

The tribal rites had all been observed, and the usual summer festivities enjoyed to the full. The camp as it broke up divided itself in three parts, each of which had determined to seek a favorite hunting-ground.

One band journeyed west, toward the Tongue River. One followed a tributary of the Powder to the south. The third merely changed camp, on account of the grazing for ponies, and for four days remained near the old place.

The party that went west did not fail to realize the perilous nature of their wanderings, for they were trespassing upon the country of the warlike Crows.

On the third day at sunrise, the Sioux crier's voice resounded in the valley of the Powder, announcing that the lodges must be razed and the villagers must take up their march.

Breakfast of jerked buffalo meat had been served and the women were adjusting their packs, not without much chatter and apparent confusion. Weeko (Beautiful Woman), the young wife of the war-chief Shunkaska, who had made many presents at the dances in honor of her twin boys, now gave one of her remaining ponies to a poor old woman whose only beast of burden, a large dog, had died during the night.

This made it necessary to shift the packs of the others. Nakpa, or Long Ears, her kittenlike gray mule, which had heretofore been honored with the precious burden of the twin babies, was to be given a heavier and more cumbersome load. Weeko's two-year-old spotted pony was selected to carry the babies.

Accordingly, the two children, in their gorgeously beaded buckskin hoods, were suspended upon either side of the pony's saddle. As Weeko's first-born, they were beautifully dressed; even the saddle and bridle were daintily worked by her own hands.

The caravan was now in motion, and Weeko started all her ponies after the leader, while she adjusted the mule's clumsy burden of kettles and other household gear. In a moment:

"Go on, let us see how you move with your new load! Go on!" she exclaimed again, with a light blow of the horse-hair lariat, as the animal stood perfectly still.

Nakpa simply gave an angry side glance at her load and shifted her position once or twice. Then she threw herself headlong into the air and landed stiff-legged, uttering at the same time her unearthly protest. First she dove straight through the crowd, then proceeded in a circle, her heels describing wonderful curves and sweeps in the air. Her pack, too, began to come to pieces and to take forced flights from her undignified body and heels, in the midst of the screams of women and children, the barking of dogs, and the war-whoops of the amused young braves.

The cowskin tent became detached from her saddle, and a moment later Nakpa stood free. Her sides worked like a bellows as she stood there meekly indignant, apparently considering herself to be the victim of an uncalled-for misunderstanding.

"I should put an arrow through her at once, only she is not worth a good arrow," said Shunkaska, or White Dog, the husband of Weeko. At his wife's answer, he opened his eyes in surprised displeasure.

"No, she shall have her own pack again. She wants her twins. I ought never to have taken them from her!"

Weeko approached Nakpa as she stood alone and unfriended in the face of her little world, all of whom considered that she had committed the unpardonable sin. As for her, she evidently felt that her misfortunes had not been of her own making. She gave a hesitating, sidelong look at her mistress.

"Nakpa, you should not have acted so. I knew you were stronger than the others, therefore I gave you that load," said Weeko in a conciliatory tone, and patted her on the nose. "Come, now, you shall have your own pet pack," and she led her back to where the young pony stood silently with the babies.

Nakpa threw back her ears and cast savage looks at him, while Shunkaska, with no small annoyance, gathered together as much as he could of their scattered household effects. The sleeping brown-skinned babies in their chrysalis-like hoods were gently lowered from the pony's back and attached securely to Nakpa's padded wooden saddle. The family pots and kettles were divided among the pack ponies. Order was restored and the village once more in motion.

"Come now, Nakpa; you have your wish. You must take good care of my babies. Be good, because I have trusted you," murmured the young mother in her softest tones.

"Really, Weeko, you have some common ground with Nakpa, for you both always want to have your own way, and stick to it, too! I tell you, I fear this Long Ears. She is not to be trusted with babies," remarked Shunkaska, with a good deal of severity. But his wife made no reply, for she well knew that though he might criticise, he would not actually interfere with her domestic arrangements.

He now started ahead to join the men in advance of the slow-moving procession, thus leaving her in undivided charge of her household. One or two of the pack ponies were not well-trained and required all her attention. Nakpa had been a faithful servant until her escapade of the morning, and she was now obviously satisfied with her mistress' arrangements. She walked alongside with her lariat dragging, and perfectly free to do as she pleased.

Some hours later, the party ascended a slope from the river bottom to cross over the divide which lay between the Powder River and a tributary stream. They had hitherto followed that river in a westerly direction, but here it took its course southward, winding in a blue streak until lost to view among the foot-hills of the Big Horn Mountains. The ford was deep, with a swift current. Here and there a bald butte stood out in full relief against the brilliant blue sky. The Sioux followed a deep ravine until they came almost up to the second row of terraces.

"Whoo! whoo!" came the blood-curdling signal of danger from the front. It was no unfamiliar sound—the rovers knew it only too well. It meant sudden death—or at best a cruel struggle and frantic flight.

Terrified, yet self-possessed, the women turned to fly while yet there was time. Instantly the mother looked to Nakpa, who carried on either side of the saddle her precious boys. She hurriedly examined the fastenings to see that all was secure, and then caught her swiftest pony, for, like all Indian women, she knew just what was happening, and that while her husband was engaged in front with the enemy, she must seek safety with her babies.

Hardly was she in the saddle when a heartrending war-whoop sounded on their flank, and she knew that they were surrounded! Instinctively she reached for her husband's second quiver of arrows, which was carried by one of the pack ponies. Alas! the Crow warriors were already upon them! The ponies became unmanageable, and the wild screams of women and children pierced the awful confusion.

Quick as a flash, Weeko turned again to her babies, but Nakpa had already disappeared!

Then, maddened by fright and the loss of her children, Weeko became forgetful of her sex and tenderness, for she sternly grasped her husband's bow in her left hand to do battle.

That charge of the Crows was a disastrous one, but the Sioux were equally brave and desperate. Charges and counter-charges were made, and the slain were many on both sides. The fight lasted until darkness came. Then the Crows departed and the Sioux buried their dead.

When the Crows made their flank charge, Nakpa apparently appreciated the situation. To save herself and the babies, she took a desperate chance. She fled straight through the attacking force.

When the warriors came howling upon her in great numbers, she at once started back the way she had come, to the camp left behind. They had traveled nearly three days. To be sure, they did not travel more than fifteen miles a day, but it was full forty miles to cover before dark.

"Look! look!" exclaimed a warrior, "two babies hung from the saddle of a mule!"

No one heeded this man's call, and his arrow did not touch Nakpa or either of the boys, but it struck the thick part of the saddle over the mule's back.

"Lasso her! lasso her!" he yelled once more; but Nakpa was too cunning for them. She dodged in and out with active heels, and they could not afford to waste many arrows on a mule at that stage of the fight. Down the ravine, then over the expanse of prairie dotted with gray-green sage-brush, she sped with her unconscious burden.

"Whoo! whoo!" yelled another Crow to his comrades, "the Sioux have dispatched a runner to get reinforcements! There he goes, down on the flat! Now he has almost reached the river bottom!"

It was only Nakpa. She laid back her cars and stretched out more and more to gain the river, for she realized that when she had crossed the ford the Crows would not pursue her farther.

Now she had reached the bank. With the intense heat from her exertions, she was extremely nervous, and she imagined a warrior behind every bush. Yet she had enough sense left to realize that she must not satisfy her thirst. She tried the bottom with her fore-foot, then waded carefully into the deep stream.

She kept her big ears well to the front as she swam to catch the slightest sound. As she stepped on the opposite shore, she shook herself and the boys vigorously, then pulled a few mouthfuls of grass and started on.

Soon one of the babies began to cry, and the other was not long in joining him. Nakpa did not know what to do. She gave a gentle whinny and both babies apparently stopped to listen; then she took up an easy gait as if to put them to sleep.

These tactics answered only for a time. As she fairly flew over the lowlands, the babies' hunger increased and they screamed so loud that a passing coyote had to sit upon his haunches and wonder what in the world the fleeing longeared horse was carrying on his saddle. Even magpies and crows flew near as if to ascertain the meaning of this curious sound.

Nakpa now came to the Little Trail Creek, a tributary of the Powder, not far from the old camp. No need of wasting any time here, she thought. Then she swerved aside so suddenly as almost to jerk her babies out of their cradles. Two gray wolves, one on each side, approached her, growling low—their white teeth showing.

Never in her humble life had Nakpa been in more desperate straits. The larger of the wolves came fiercely forward to engage her attention, while his mate was to attack her behind and cut her hamstrings. But for once the pair had made a miscalculation. The mule used her front hoofs vigorously on the foremost wolf, while her hind ones were doing even more effective work. The larger wolf soon went limping away with a broken hip, and the one in the rear received a deep cut on the jaw which proved an effectual discouragement.

A little further on, an Indian hunter drew near on horseback, but Nakpa did not pause or slacken her pace. On she fled through the long dry grass of the river bottoms, while her babies slept again from sheer exhaustion. Toward sunset, she entered the Sioux camp amid great excitement, for some one had spied her afar off, and the boys and the dogs announced her coming.

"Whoo, whoo! Weeko's Nakpa has come back with the twins! Whoo, whoo!" exclaimed the men. "Tokee! tokee!" cried the women.

A sister to Weeko who was in the village came forward and released the children, as Nakpa gave a low whinny and stopped. Tenderly Zeezeewin nursed them at her own motherly bosom, assisted by another young mother of the band.

"Ugh, there is a Crow arrow sticking in the saddle! A fight! a fight!" exclaimed the warriors.

"Sing a Brave-Heart song for the Long-Eared one! She has escaped alone with her charge. She is entitled to wear an eagle's feather! Look at the arrow in her saddle! and more, she has a knife wound in her jaw and an arrow cut on her hind leg.—No, those are the marks of a wolf's teeth! She has passed through many dangers and saved two chief's sons, who will some day make the Crows sorry for this day's work!"

The speaker was an old man who thus addressed the fast gathering throng.

Zeezeewin now came forward again with an eagle feather and some white paint in her hands. The young men rubbed Nakpa down, and the feather, marked with red to indicate her wounds, was fastened to her mane. Shoulders and hips were touched with red paint to show her endurance in running. Then the crier, praising her brave deed in heroic verse, led her around the camp, inside of the circle of teepees. All the people stood outside their lodges and listened respectfully, for the Dakota loves well to honor the faithful and the brave.

During the next day, riders came in from the ill-fated party, bringing the sad news of the fight and heavy loss. Late in the afternoon came Weeko, her face swollen with crying, her beautiful hair cut short in mourning, her garments torn and covered with dust and blood. Her husband had fallen in the fight, and her twin boys she supposed to have been taken captive by the Crows. Singing in a hoarse voice the praises of her departed warrior, she entered the camp. As she approached her sister's teepee, there stood Nakpa, still wearing her honorable decorations. At the same moment, Zeezeewin came out to meet her with both babies in her arms.

"Mechinkshee! meechinkshee! (my sons, my sons!)" was all that the poor mother could say, as she all but fell from her saddle to the ground. The despised Long Ears had not betrayed her trust.

VIII
THE WAR MAIDEN

The old man, Smoky Day, was for many years the best-known story-teller and historian of his tribe. He it was who told me the story of the War Maiden. In the old days it was unusual but not unheard of for a woman to go upon the war-path—perhaps a young girl, the last of her line, or a widow whose well-loved husband had fallen on the field—and there could be no greater incentive to feats of desperate daring on the part of the warriors. "A long time ago," said old Smoky Day, "the Unkpapa and the Cut-Head bands of Sioux united their camps upon a vast prairie east of the Minne Wakan (now called Devil's Lake). It was midsummer, and the people shared in the happiness of every living thing. We had food in abundance, for bison in countless numbers overspread the plain.

"The teepee village was laid out in two great rings, and all was in readiness for the midsummer entertainments. There were ball games, feasts and dances every day, and late into the night. You have heard of the festivities of those days; there are none like them now," said the old man, and he sighed heavily as he laid down the red pipe which was to be passed from hand to hand during the recital.

"The head chief of the Unkpapas then was Tamakoche (His Country). He was in his time a notable warrior, a hunter and a feastmaker, much beloved by his people. He was the father of three sons, but he was so anxious to make them warriors of great reputation that they had all, despising danger, been killed in battle.

"The chief had also a very pretty daughter, whose name was Makatah. Since all his sons were slain he had placed his affections solely upon the girl, and she grew up listening to the praises of the brave deeds of her brothers, which her father never tired of chanting when they were together in the lodge. At times Makatah was called upon to dance to the 'Strong-Heart' songs. Thus even as a child she loved the thought of war, although she was the prettiest and most modest maiden in the two tribes. As she grew into womanhood she became the belle of her father's village, and her beauty and spirit were talked of even among the neighboring bands of Sioux. But it appeared that Makatah did not care to marry. She had only two ambitions. One was to prove to her father that, though only a maid, she had the heart of a warrior. The other was to visit the graves of her brothers—that is, the country of the enemy.

"At this pleasant reunion of two kindred peoples one of the principal events was the Feast of Virgins, given by Makatah. All young maidens of virtue and good repute were invited to be present; but woe to her who should dare to pollute the sacred feast! If her right to be there were challenged by any it meant a public disgrace. The two arrows and the red stone upon which the virgins took their oath of chastity were especially prepared for the occasion. Every girl was beautifully dressed, for at that time the white doeskin gowns, with a profusion of fringes and colored embroidery, were the gala attire of the Sioux maidens. Red paint was added, and ornaments of furs and wampum. Many youths eagerly surveyed the maiden gathering, at which the daughter of Tamakoche outshone all the rest.

"Several eligible warriors now pressed their suits at the chieftain's lodge, and among them were one or two whom he would have gladly called son-in-law; but no! Makatah would not listen to words of courtship. She had vowed, she said, to the spirits of her three brothers—each of whom fell in the country of the Crows—that she would see that country before she became a wife.

"Red Horn, who was something of a leader among the young men, was a persistent and determined suitor. He had urged every influential friend of his and hers to persuade her to listen to him. His presents were more valuable than those of any one else. He even made use of his father's position as a leading chief of the Cut-Head band to force a decision in his favor; and while the maiden remained indifferent her father seemed inclined to countenance this young man's pretensions.

"She had many other lovers, as I have said," the old man added, "and among them was one Little Eagle, an orphan and a poor young man, unknown and unproved as a warrior. He was so insignificant that nobody thought much about him, and if Makatah regarded him with any favor the matter was her secret, for it is certain that she did not openly encourage him.

"One day it was reported in the village that their neighbors, the Cut-Head Sioux, would organize a great attack upon the Crows at the mouth of the Redwater, a tributary of the Missouri. Makatah immediately inquired of her male cousins whether any of them expected to join the war-party.

"'Three of us will go,' they replied.

"'Then,' said the girl, 'I beg that you will allow me to go with you! I have a good horse, and I shall not handicap you in battle. I only ask your protection in camp as your kinswoman and a maid of the war-party.'

"'If our uncle Tamakoche sanctions your going,' they replied, 'we shall be proud to have our cousin with us, to inspire us to brave deeds!'

"The maiden now sought her father and asked his permission to accompany the warparty

"'I wish,' said she, 'to visit the graves of my brothers! I shall carry with me their war-bonnets and their weapons, to give to certain young men on the eve of battle, according to the ancient custom. Long ago I resolved to do this, and the time is now come.'

"The chief was at this time well advanced in years, and had been sitting quite alone in his lodge, thinking upon the days of his youth, when he was noted for daring and success in battle. In silence he listened as he filled his pipe, and seemed to meditate while he smoked the fragrant tobacco. At last he spoke with tears in his eyes.

"'Daughter, I am an old man! My heart beats in my throat, and my old eyes cannot keep back the tears. My three sons, on whom I had placed all my hopes, are gone to a far country! You are the only child left to my old age, and you, too, are brave—as brave as any of your brothers. If you go I fear that you may not return to me; yet I cannot refuse you my permission!"

"The old man began to chant a war-song, and some of his people, hearing him, came in to learn what was in his mind. He told them all, and immediately many young men volunteered for the war-party, in order to have the honor of going with the daughter of their chief.

"Several of Makatah's suitors were among them, and each watched eagerly for an opportunity to ride at her side. At night she pitched her little teepee within the circle of her cousins' campfires, and there she slept without fear. Courteous youths brought to her every morning and evening fresh venison for her repast. Yet there was no courting, for all attentions paid to a maiden when on the war-path must be those of a brother to a sister, and all must be equally received by her.

"Two days later, when the two parties of Sioux met on the plains, the maiden's presence was heralded throughout the camp, as an inspiration to the young and untried warriors of both bands to distinguish themselves in the field. It is true that some of the older men considered it unwise to allow Makatah to accompany the war-party.

"'The girl,' said they to one another, 'is very ambitious as well as brave. She will surely risk her own life in battle, which will make the young men desperate, and we shall lose many of them!'

"Nevertheless they loved her and her father; therefore they did not protest openly.

"On the third day the Sioux scouts returned with the word that the Crows were camping, as had been supposed, at the confluence of the Redwater and the Missouri Rivers. It was a great camp. All the Crow tribe were there, they said, with their thousands of fine horses.

"There was excitement in the Sioux camp, and all of the head men immediately met in council. It was determined to make the attack early on the following morning, just as the sun came over the hills. The councilors agreed that in honor of the great chief, her father, as well as in recognition of her own courage, Makatah should be permitted to lead the charge at the outset, but that she must drop behind as they neared the enemy. The maiden, who had one of the fleetest ponies in that part of the country, had no intention of falling back, but she did not tell any one what was in her mind.

"That evening every warrior sang his warsong, and announced the particular war-charm or 'medicine' of his clan, according to the custom. The youths were vying with one another in brave tales of what they would do on the morrow. The voice of Red Horn was loud among the boasters, for he was known to be a vain youth, although truly not without reputation. Little Eagle, who was also of the company, remained modestly silent, as indeed became one without experience in the field. In the midst of the clamor there fell a silence.

"'Hush! hush!' they whispered. 'Look, look! The War Maiden comes!'

"All eyes were turned upon Makatah, who rode her fine buckskin steed with a single lariat. He held his head proudly, and his saddle was heavy with fringes and gay with colored embroidery. The maiden was attired in her best and wore her own father's war-bonnet, while she carried in her hands two which had belonged to two of her dead brothers. Singing in a clear voice the songs of her clan, she completed the circle, according to custom, before she singled out one of the young braves for special honor by giving him the bonnet which she held in her right hand. She then crossed over to the Cut-Heads, and presented the other bonnet to one of their young men. She was very handsome; even the old men's blood was stirred by her brave appearance!

"At daybreak the two war-parties of the Sioux, mounted on their best horses, stood side by side, ready for the word to charge. All of the warriors were painted for the battle—prepared for death—their nearly nude bodies decorated with their individual war-totems. Their well-filled quivers were fastened to their sides, and each tightly grasped his oaken bow.

"The young man with the finest voice had been chosen to give the signal—a single highpitched yell. This was an imitation of the one long howl of the gray wolf before he makes the attack. It was an ancient custom of our people.

"'Woo-o-o-o!'—at last it came! As the sound ceased a shrill war-whoop from five hundred throats burst forth in chorus, and at the same instant Makatah, upon her splendid buckskin pony, shot far out upon the plain, like an arrow as it leaves the bow. It was a glorious sight! No man has ever looked upon the like again!"

The eyes of the old man sparkled as he spoke, and his bent shoulders straightened.

"The white doeskin gown of the War Maiden," he continued, "was trimmed with elk's teeth and tails of ermine. Her long black hair hung loose, bound only with a strip of otter-skin, and with her eagle-feather war-bonnet floated far behind. In her hand she held a long coup-staff decorated with eagle-feathers. Thus she went forth in advance of them all!

"War cries of men and screams of terrified women and children were borne upon the clear morning air as our warriors neared the Crow camp. The charge was made over a wide plain, and the Crows came yelling from their lodges, fully armed, to meet the attacking party. In spite of the surprise they easily held their own, and even began to press us hard, as their number was much greater than that of the Sioux.

"The fight was a long and hard one. Toward the end of the day the enemy made a counter-charge. By that time many of our ponies had fallen or were exhausted. The Sioux retreated, and the slaughter was great. The Cut-Heads fled womanlike; but the people of Tamakoche fought gallantly to the very last.

"Makatah remained with her father's people. Many cried out to her, 'Go back! Go back!' but she paid no attention. She carried no weapon throughout the day—nothing but her coup-staff—but by her presence and her cries of encouragement or praise she urged on the men to deeds of desperate valor.

"Finally, however, the Sioux braves were hotly pursued and the retreat became general. Now at last Makatah tried to follow; but her pony was tired, and the maiden fell farther and farther behind. Many of her lovers passed her silently, intent upon saving their own lives. Only a few still remained behind, fighting desperately to cover the retreat, when Red Horn came up with the girl. His pony was still fresh. He might have put her up behind him and carried her to safety, but he did not even look at her as he galloped by.

"Makatah did not call out, but she could not help looking after him. He had declared his love for her more loudly than any of the others, and she now gave herself up to die.

"Presently another overtook the maiden. It was Little Eagle, unhurt and smiling.

"'Take my horse!' he said to her. 'I shall remain here and fight!'

"The maiden looked at him and shook her head, but he sprang off and lifted her upon his horse. He struck him a smart blow upon the flank that sent him at full speed in the direction of the Sioux encampment. Then he seized the exhausted buckskin by the lariat, and turned back to join the rear-guard.

"That little group still withstood in some fashion the all but irresistible onset of the Crows. When their comrade came back to them, leading the War Maiden's pony, they were inspired to fresh endeavor, and though few in number they made a counter-charge with such fury that the Crows in their turn were forced to retreat!

"The Sioux got fresh mounts and returned to the field, and by sunset the day was won! Little Eagle was among the first who rode straight through the Crow camp, causing terror and consternation. It was afterward remembered that he looked unlike his former self and was scarcely recognized by the warriors for the modest youth they had so little regarded.

"It was this famous battle which drove that warlike nation, the Crows, to go away from the Missouri and to make their home up the Yellowstone River and in the Bighorn country. But many of our men fell, and among them the brave Little Eagle!

"The sun was almost over the hills when the Sioux gathered about their campfires, recounting the honors won in battle, and naming the brave dead. Then came the singing of dirges and weeping for the slain! The sadness of loss was mingled with exultation.

"Hush! listen! the singing and wailing have ceased suddenly at both camps. There is one voice coming around the circle of campfires. It is the voice of a woman! Stripped of all her ornaments, her dress shorn of its fringes, her ankles bare, her hair cropped close to her neck, leading a pony with mane and tail cut short, she is mourning as widows mourn. It is Makatah!

"Publicly, with many tears, she declared herself the widow of the brave Little Eagle, although she had never been his wife! He it was, she said with truth, who had saved her people's honor and her life at the cost of his own. He was a true man!

"'Ho, ho!' was the response from many of the older warriors; but the young men, the lovers of Makatah, were surprised and sat in silence.

"The War Maiden lived to be a very old woman, but she remained true to her vow. She never accepted a husband; and all her lifetime she was known as the widow of the brave Little Eagle."

GLOSSARY

A-no-ka-san, white on both sides (Bald Eagle).

A-tay, father.

Cha-ton'-ska, White Hawk.

Chin-o-te-dah, Lives-in-the-Wood.

Chin-to, yes, indeed.

E-na-ka-nee, hurry.

E-ya-tonk-a-wee, She-whose-Voice-is-heard-afar.

E-yo-tank-a, rise up, or sit down.

Ha-ha-ton-wan, Ojibway.

Ha-na-ka-pe, a grave.

Han-ta-wo, Out of the way!

He-che-tu, it is well.

He-yu-pe-ya, come here!

Hi! an exclamation of thanks.

Hunk-pa-tees, a band of Sioux.

Ka-po-sia, Light Lodges, a band of Sioux.

Ke-chu-wa, darling.

Ko-da, friend.

Ma-ga-ska-wee, Swan Maiden.

Ma-ka-tah, Earth Woman.

Ma-to, bear.

Ma-to-ska, White Bear.

Ma-to-sa-pa, Black Bear.

Me-chink-she, my son or sons.

Me-ta, my.

Min-ne-wa-kan, Sacred Water (Devil's Lake.)

Min-ne-ya-ta, By-the-Water.

Nak-pa, Ears or Long Ears.

Ne-na e-ya-ya! run fast!

O-glu-ge-chan-a, Mysterious Wood-Dweller.

Psay, snow-shoes.

Shunk-a, dog.

Shunk-a-ska, White Dog.

Shunk-ik-chek-a, domestic dog.

Ske-ske-ta-tonk-a, Sault Sainte Marie.

Sna-na, Rattle.

Sta-su, Shield (Arickaree).

Ta-ake-che-ta, his soldier.

Ta-chin-cha-la, fawn.

Tak-cha, doe.

Ta-lu-ta, Scarlet.

Ta-ma-hay, Pike.

Ta-ma-ko-che, His Country.

Ta-na-ge-la, Humming-Bird.

Ta-tank-a-o-ta, Many Buffaloes.

Ta-te-yo-pa, Her Door.

Ta-to-ka, Antelope.

Ta-wa-su-o-ta, Many Hailstones.

Tee-pee, tent.

Te-yo-tee-pee, Council lodge.

To-ke-ya nun-ka hu-wo? where are you?

Tunk-a-she-dah, grandfather.

Un-chee-dah, grandmother.

Unk-pa-pa, a band of Sioux.

U-ya-yo! come here!

Wa-ba-shaw, Red Hat (name of a Sioux chief).

Wa-ha-dah, Buyer of Furs.

Wah-pay-ton, a band of Sioux.

Wa-ho, Howler.

Wa-kan, sacred, mysterious.

Wak-pay-ku-tay, a band of Sioux.

Wa-pay-na, Little Barker.

Wee-ko, Beautiful Woman.

We-no-na, Firstborn Daughter.

We-sha-wee, Red Girl.

We-wop-tay, a sharpened pole.

We-yan-na, little woman.

We-zee, Smoky Lodge.

Yank-ton-nais, a band of Sioux.

Zee-zee-win, Yellow Woman.

Zu-ya-ma-ni, Walks-to-War.